Dear Writer,

Because, yes, if you're opening this journal, you're a writer. A real one. And I will address you with the respect you are due!

That said, Writer, I love opening a new journal. Every time I begin one I write a letter on the very first page, addressed to the journal itself; it is my way of preparing the pages for what's coming and of preparing myself mentally to submit to the process of putting my ideas out of my body. It is a scary, humbling, and thrilling journey to imagine a moment, image, or experience and then ascribe language to make sense of it all.

And indeed, for me, writing is a way to make sense. To grab all the jumbled feelings and ideas and current events, and historical ones too, and write *through* what initially compelled me. Writing is thinking. It is feeling. Sometimes I don't even know what I believe about a topic until I get to the end of a poem I'm drafting and realize "Ah. *This* is where it's all been leading to. This is where I didn't know I needed to arrive, but thank goodness I'm here." Because the moment I find language that accurately describes what I think and feel, it's like I've unlocked something that helps me better understand myself.

I don't want to get too mystical—or apply any pressure. But I do want to leave you with my hope for you and this journal: that it gives you the courage to give *yourself* the permission to wonder, dream, question, and maybe even share your work. Or maybe not. Whatever you do between these pages is more than enough. And so is your writing. And so are you.

Pa'lante siempre,
Liz

www.epicreads.com

ISBN 978-0-06-298227-8

Typography by Erin Fitzsimmons
19 20 21 22 23 SCP 10 9 8 7 6 5 4 3 2 1

❖

First Edition

# WRITE yourself a LANTERN

## A JOURNAL
### inspired by THE POET X
#### BY
## ELIZABETH ACEVEDO

**HARPER**
*An Imprint of HarperCollinsPublishers*

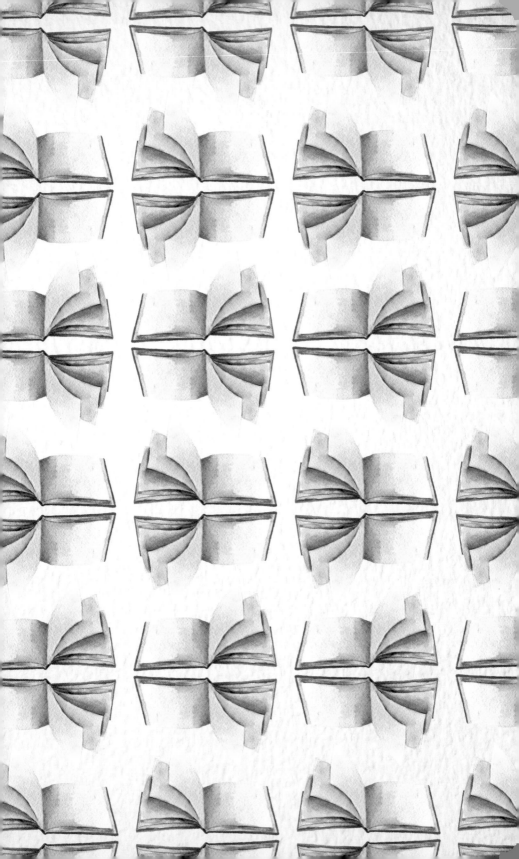

I'VE FORCED MY SKIN JUST AS THICK AS I AM.

# PERO,

## tú no

## eres

# FÁCIL.

# WRITE ABOUT THE MOST IMPACTFUL DAY OF YOUR LIFE.

_____

_____

_____

_____

_____

_____

_____

_____

_____

_____

_____

I've been HAVING all these FEELINGS.

_____

_____

_____

_____

_____

_____

_____

_____

_____

_____

_____

_____

_____

_____

_____

_____

_____

*I feel* TOO SMALL
*for all that's*
INSIDE ME.

EVEN BEFORE
this DAY
I think I've been
BEGINNING.

"Mira,
muchacha"

IF MEDUSA *was* DOMINICAN *and had a* DAUGHTER, I THINK I'D BE HER.

# I LOOK and FEEL like a MYTH.

_____

_____

_____

_____

_____

_____

_____

_____

_____

_____

_____

_____

_____

_____

_____

Make
POEMS
from the
SHARP
FEELINGS
inside.

# WRITE THE LAST PARAGRAPHS OF YOUR BIOGRAPHY.

_____

_____

_____

_____

_____

_____

_____

_____

_____

_____

_____

_____

_____

_____

# CALLING ALL POETS!

_____
_____
_____
_____
_____
_____
_____
_____
_____
_____
_____
_____
_____
_____
_____
_____

"This
WORLD'S
been waiting
FOR YOUR
GENIUS
for a
LONG
TIME."

I let my
BODY
finally
TAKE UP
all the
SPACE
it WANTS.

I let the **WORDS**
**SHAPE** themselves **HARD**
on my **TONGUE**.

A STUDENT,
a MIRACLE,
a protective SISTER,
a misunderstood
DAUGHTER

I am **LOOSE** and **BLANK PAGES.**

She SHOULD be REMEMBERED as always WORKING to become the WARRIOR she WANTED TO BE.

# POEMS build inside ME.

IT BE
GIBBERISH
but
EVERYTHING
you
WHISPER
sounds like
POETRY.

"You got bars, X."

This was
SUPPOSED
to be a
QUESTION.
Not a POEM
CONFESSION or
WHATEVER
it's become.

WORDS . . .

_____

_____

_____

_____

_____

_____

_____

_____

_____

_____

_____

_____

_____

_____

_____

_____

_____

_____

*more* **HEAT** *like* **NOTHING ELSE.**

# DESCRIBE SOMEONE YOU CONSIDER MISUNDERSTOOD BY SOCIETY.

_____
_____
_____
_____
_____
_____
_____
_____
_____
_____
_____
_____
_____

Write
something
BEAUTIFUL
for
YOURSELF.

The SOUND
of our HEARTBEATS

There was
FREEDOM
there,
in
FLYING.

_____

_____

_____

_____

_____

_____

_____

_____

_____

_____

_____

_____

_____

## It's BEAUTIFUL
### and REAL and what I wanted.

There is

# FREEDOM

in choosing

to SiT and

be STiLL.

The MOTH
always seeks the
LIGHT.

"Who woulda THOUGHT you was a POET? DOPE."

That girl's a
STORYTELLER
writing a
WORLD
you're invited
to WALK INTO.

_____

_____

_____

_____

_____

_____

_____

_____

_____

_____

_____

_____

_____

_____

AT LEAST *there's* POETRY.

I'm like a
HAIKU
with different
SIDES.

# WHEN WAS THE LAST TIME YOU FELT FREE?

_____

_____

_____

_____

_____

_____

_____

_____

_____

_____

_____

_____

_____

# "just let us hear every WORD."

The
PAGES
of my
notebook
SWELL.

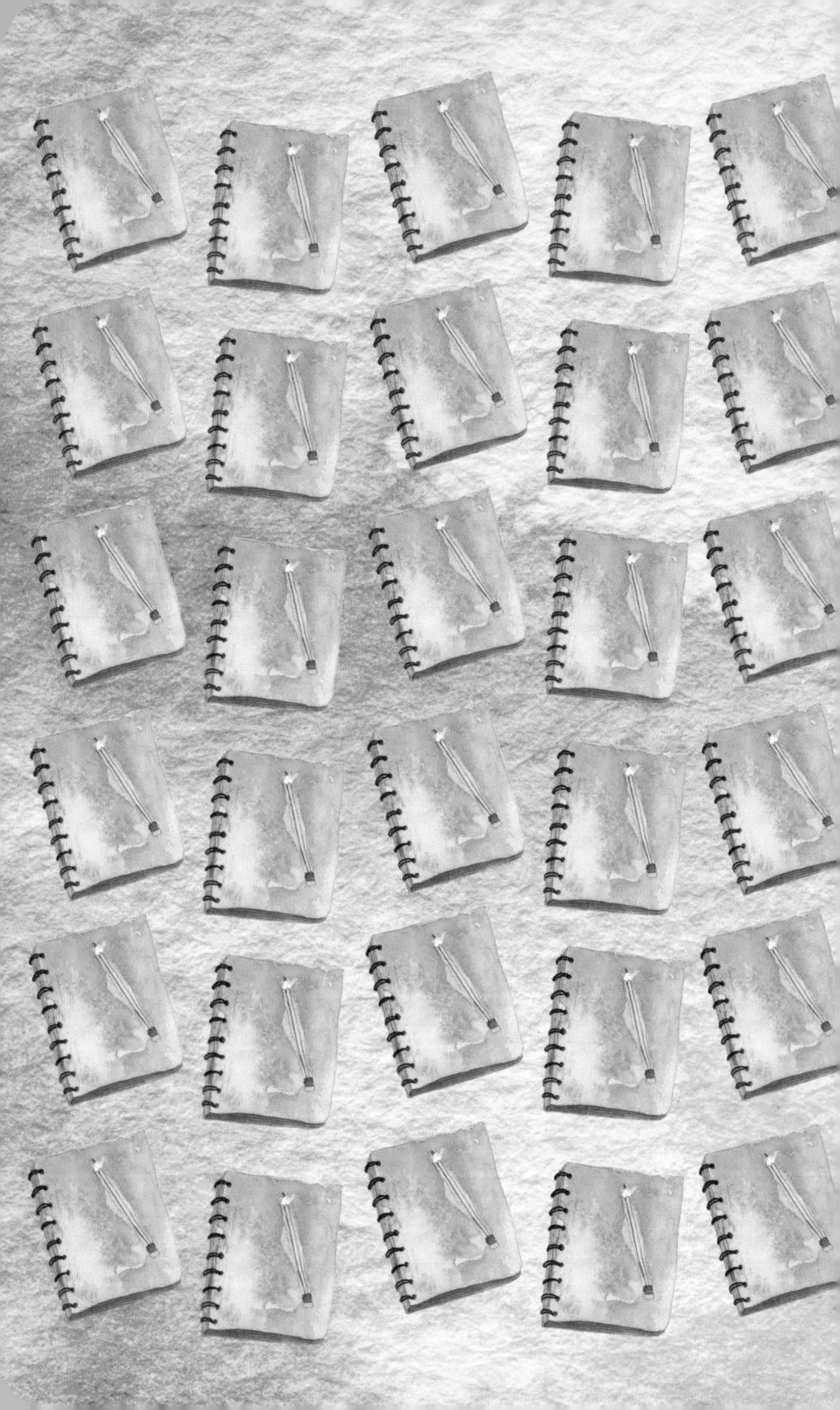

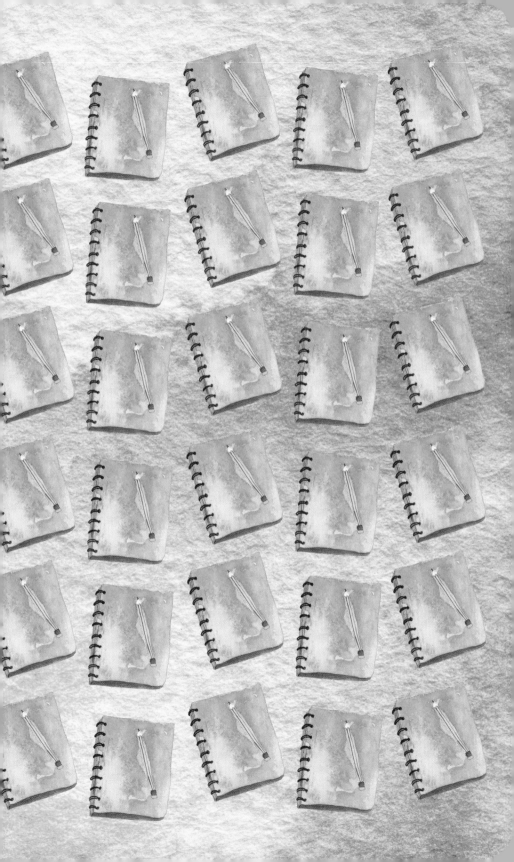

The more
I BRUISE the
PAGE
the quicker
something
inside me
HEALS.

HOPE *flies quick into*
*my* BODY'S *corners.*

My WORDS,
my thoughts,
the ONLY PLACE
I have ever
been my
whole SELF . . . .

When has anyone EVER TOLD me I HAD the RIGHT TO STOP iT ALL without MY KNUCKLES, or MY ANGER, with just SOME SIMPLE WORDS.

But
OUR ARMS
can do
what our
WORDS CAN'T
just now.

_____

_____

_____

_____

_____

_____

_____

_____

_____

_____

_____

_____

_____

_____

_____

I let the **WORDS** carry me away.

# WORDS
give people
# PERMISSION
to be their
# FULLEST
# SELF.

# EXPLAIN YOUR FAVORITE QUOTE.

# THE POETRY'S CLUB'S REAL RULES OF SLAM:

1. PERFORM with HEART

2. REMEMBER why you WROTE the POEM

3. GO in with all YOUR EMOTIONS

4. TELL the AUDIENCE ALL OF THE things

5. DON'T SUCK

Say SOMETHING,

_____

_____

_____

_____

_____

_____

_____

_____

_____

_____

_____

_____

_____

_____

_____

_____

_____

**ANYTHING.**

THE FIRST
WORDS OF
THE POEM
*unwrinkle*
THEMSELVES.

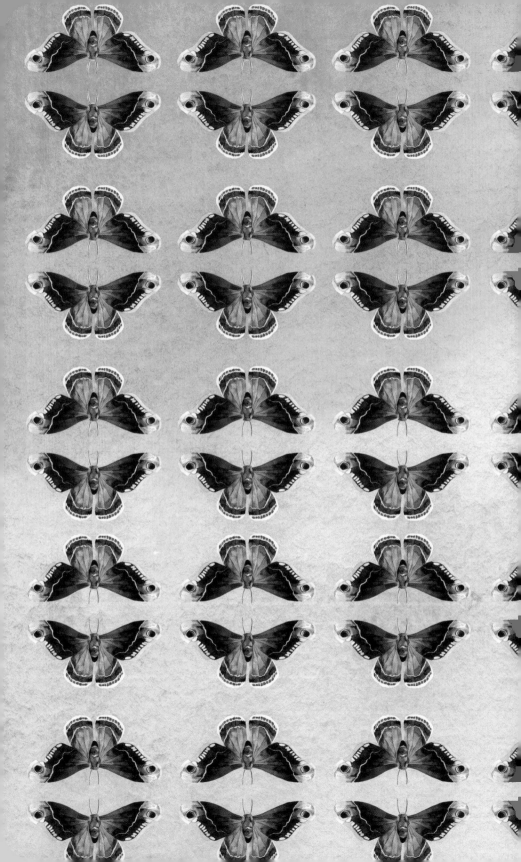

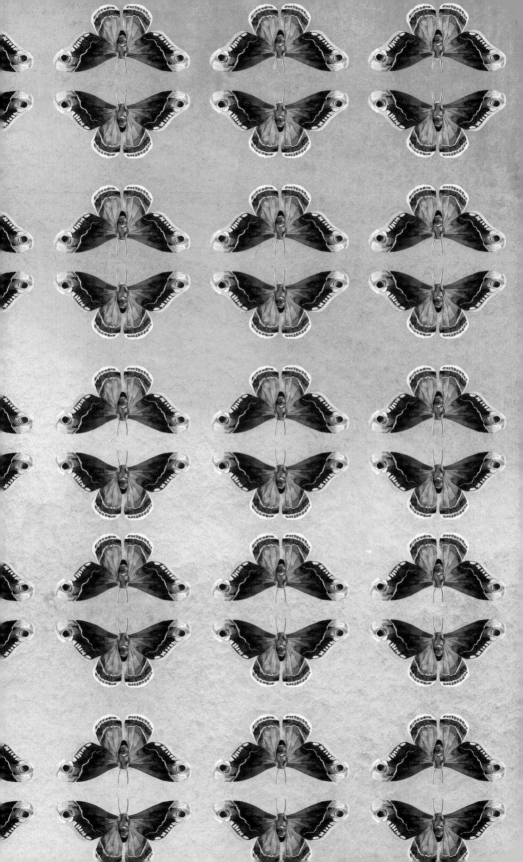

"I'll ALWAYS
have your
BACK,
and I'll
ALWAYS
protect your
HEART."

_____

_____

_____

_____

_____

_____

_____

_____

_____

_____

_____

_____

_____

_____

_____

_____

We both have
SECRETS to KEEP.

"DANCING is a GOOD WAY to tell someone you LOVE THEM."

_____

_____

_____

_____

_____

_____

_____

_____

_____

_____

_____

_____

_____

_____

_____

The more I WRITE
the BRAVER I become.

AND ISN'T THAT
WHAT A **POEM** IS?

*A lantern*

*glowing*

*in the dark.*

I SMILE
at them
both and
STEP
FORWARD.

But my POEMS?
They're about ME.

_____

_____

_____

_____

_____

_____

_____

_____

_____

_____

_____

_____

_____

_____

_____

There is POWER in the WORD.